# Stop Smoking

Strategies For Quitting Smoking And Achieving A Smoke-Free Lifestyle For Enhanced Well-being

*(Reclaiming Control Over Your Life From Nicotine Addiction: A Guide To Permanently Ceasing Smoking)*

**Ron Martel**

# TABLE OF CONTENT

Getting Rid Of The Addiction .......................................... 1

Utilizing Optimism For Achieving Desired Outcomes .......................................... 8

How Do You Be Positive? ......................................... 12

How To Strategically Engage With The Opposing Force ............................................. 25

How To Manage Your Cravings ............................. 35

Allow Us To Collaborate In Discovering Your Fundamental Purpose. ............................................. 71

Quit Smoking Benefit ............................................. 102

Embrace The Impetus To Cease Smoking ...... 108

Why Do We Smoke? ................................................ 126

## Getting Rid Of The Addiction

Finding inner strength

Currently, I possess a level of strength unparalleled by any previous point in my existence. I possess accurate knowledge of my preferences and aversions. If I were to receive another unexpected phone call, I am fully confident and determined that I would not resume the habit of smoking harmful tobacco products. I possess authority over the entirety of my existence. I have always maintained the awareness of possessing superior abilities. I reflected upon it on each occasion that I brought a cigarette to my lips.

You possess far greater qualities than your habit. Personally, I have not resorted to using patches or nicotine-free cigarettes. I became acutely aware of my intrinsic worth, recognizing that my presence on this planet held profound significance, and I refused to allow cigarettes to undermine my divine calling. I approached the situation with a day-by-day outlook and firmly resolved within myself that I had reached my limit. There were no mystical remedies or supernatural practices at play. I have been entrusted by a divine force with a specific mission. I am on a dedicated pursuit, and no obstacles can impede my progress. The journey was arduous. I encountered significant difficulty and grappled with my physical prowess. How could I have permitted a substance to exert dominance over my being? This struggle transcends the physical realm, primarily residing as a mental confrontation. The genesis of it all resides in the realm of one's consciousness. Once one acquires an intense determination to cease smoking, they are on a promising path towards achieving a smoke-free existence. It grows progressively more effortless as time elapses.

I developed a personalized timetable and overhauled my entire regimen. This helped a lot. Before engaging in smoking, I was employed in a typical Monday-through-Friday job from 9 AM to 5 PM. I engaged in smoking prior to commencing work and anticipated my inaugural break for smoking, scheduled for 9:00 am. I was aware that my scheduled break for smoking would occur during the lunch hour, specifically at 12:00pm. The organization with which I was employed provided a designated area specifically for individuals who engage in smoking, and this locale subsequently became a popular meeting place for all staff members.

I made the conscious decision to abstain from smoking during my extended period of working on a project at home. I established a disciplined timetable supplemented by a comprehensive checklist encompassing prayer, physical exercise, adequate hydration, and engaging in productive activities throughout the day. I am not suggesting that it is necessary for you to resign from your employment in order to cease this unpleasant habit. I am simply suggesting that it would be advisable for you to contemplate modifying your current routine. If you gather discreetly with your acquaintances for smoking purposes behind the premises during the designated lunch period, such action would not be deemed acceptable.

Finding a Distraction

Developing New Habits

Additionally, it is advisable to cultivate the practice of engaging in reading. I am cognizant of your thoughts. You may possibly perceive me as irrational. What is the correlation between reading and my decision to cease smoking? It's very simple. Engaging in reading can divert your attention away from the thoughts of smoking. Recall the occasion when I advised you to modify your daily regimen and alter the locations you frequent during your breaks for smoking. Locate a designated area frequented by individuals who do not smoke, and bring along a book for your own leisure. In the event that you do not particularly enjoy the act of reading, I would highly advise you to seek out a literary work pertaining to a subject matter that captivates your interest. That is an excellent way to commence. That constitutes the most effortless method to cultivate a penchant for reading. Now that you find yourself in a distinct setting, distanced from all forms of enticement. Please obtain a glass of water and direct your attention to your book. Water aids in reducing cravings and in the event that one chooses to indulge in a cigarette subsequent to consuming a substantial amount of filtered water, the sensory experience of the tobacco product would be thoroughly unsatisfying. Water cleanses and heals. Dehydration will induce an unprecedented level of craving.

During this period, I extensively engaged with self-help literature. The literature served as a source of inspiration and provided solace during those challenging periods. I was aware that there were multiple aspects of my being that required significant improvement, including the physical, mental, emotional, and spiritual dimensions. I found myself situated neither in the desired nor the requisite location. I wanted more. Therefore, I engaged with literature that provided inspiration and fortitude. I cultivated the ability to practice self-discipline and maintain unwavering focus on my vision and aspirations. The objective was to strive for personal growth and eliminate the aspects of myself that were not aligned with my highest potential. I take great pride in my commitment to abstaining from smoking and persevering with the ongoing trajectory. It's a wonderful feeling.

## Utilizing Optimism For Achieving Desired Outcomes

Positivity forms the essence of the law of attraction. Doesn't everyone aim to avoid attracting negative factors? Hence, it can be inferred that the law of attraction revolves around harnessing the faculties of the mind or the potency of affirmative thoughts to manifest our genuine aspirations in life.

Thus, what strategy shall we employ to materialize our desired outcomes through the power of positive thinking?

Presented here are several guidelines to guarantee the attainment of your desired outcomes in life:

1. Cease the creation of undesirable circumstances and direct your attention towards the object of your desire: In accordance with the principle of the law of attraction, it is possible to draw towards yourself anything upon which you concentrate your thoughts.

Therefore, in order to prevent any unfavorable outcomes, it is advisable to refrain from contemplating such matters. Do not allow it to trouble you. It is as straightforward as that...In lieu of that, direct your attention towards your desires. Acquire the skill of managing your thoughts and directing them towards a positive orientation. Generate a favorable encounter for both your own persona and those in your immediate vicinity. Optimism is contagious. Seek to minimize the presence of negative thoughts in your mind.

2. Place trust in your abilities: Expressing your desires is a simple task. It is quite effortless to conceive our desires. Nevertheless, do we genuinely hold the conviction that this event will come to fruition? Faith wields immense strength, so much so that it is capable of effecting miracles, provided one maintains unwavering belief in their occurrence. In order to encounter the ideal individual in your life, it is imperative to maintain a steadfast belief

in the eventuality of such an encounter. To achieve happiness and success, it is imperative to adopt a mindset centered around both attainments, and harbor unwavering faith in one's ability to attain them. In order to embark on global travels, it is imperative to foster a strong conviction in your ability to achieve this feat. If you desire to achieve recuperation from your ailment, do not allow it to overpower you. Have confidence and hold the conviction in your mind that you will recover and your illness will cease to afflict you. That is the role and practice of faith healers. They assist individuals in discovering the fortitude and steadfast determination to prevail over adversities or afflictions they encounter. Once one embraces these beliefs, the process of healing occurs effortlessly, akin to a miraculous occurrence. The human intellect possesses immense prowess. It is capable of accomplishing anything it imagines. If one holds steadfast faith, it shall come to pass.

3. Alter your mindset: Do you place faith in the concept of luck? Do you believe that fortune is exclusive to a select few individuals? Well, fortune favors those who fail to recognize the importance of optimistic mindset. The concept of luck does not exist. Fortunate individuals are those who possess optimistic attitudes and a deep belief in their deservingness of favorable circumstances. They possess fortuitousness as a result of their proactive approach in capitalizing on every chance presented to them, driven by an unwavering belief in their ability to take hold of it. When one adopts such a positive attitude and perceives things optimistically, one can consider oneself fortunate indeed.

## How Do You Be Positive?

Optimism is self-imposed. It is a choice. If you make the choice to be happy, happiness can be attained. In a similar vein, fostering an optimistic mindset can enable the cultivation of a positive thinking disposition. In the event that an unusual circumstance befalls you, how would you respond? Do you elect to disregard the matter and continue living in the manner that you previously did? Alternatively, do you engage in introspection regarding the events and derive valuable lessons from them while actively seeking to extract the positive aspects of the experience? Alternatively, do you possess a proclivity to respond unfavorably and assign fault for occurrences onto others?

One's perspective on life is contingent upon oneself. If one opts not to engage in social interactions, they should not be astonished at finding themselves in solitude. If you opt to disregard your well-being, do not express discontent when you become unwell. If one possesses an affinity for life and takes pleasure in the experiences it presents, this optimistic perspective will yield favorable outcomes, leading to both happiness and success.

By adopting a positive perspective, one perceives life as abundant with solutions and opportunities. A negative perception entails perceiving it with an abundance of impediments and concerns.

Here is a strategy to cultivate a mindset of optimism and positivity:

1. Mental conditioning: The initial and foremost step in cultivating a constructive mindset is through the practice of calming the mind. If one is burdened by worries, pessimistic

thoughts, fears, and anxiety, it becomes challenging for the mind to find solace and concentration remains elusive. You must engage in relaxation techniques to calm your mind. The most effective approach to attaining this objective is through practicing meditation or engaging in yoga. When you initiate the act of closing your eyes, your sensory perception experiences a heightening effect and it becomes more manageable to direct your attention internally rather than externally. Breathe in...breathe out. When your mind achieves a state of relaxation and your body attains a state of tranquility, you will find it more facile to contemplate upon your genuine aspirations and concentrate on them. Experience the surge of vitality coursing through your being. Direct your attention to the present moment and contemplate the aspirations you aim to realize. Continue to engage in this practice consistently until it becomes a ingrained and beneficial routine.

2. Refrain from displaying a frowning expression: Embracing a smile serves as an optimal form of exercise, as it effectively engages and stretches numerous intricate nerves and muscles dispersed across the facial region. Despite any unfavorable circumstances, it is advisable to maintain a pleasant countenance. In situations where your interpersonal connections appear to be becoming unmanageable, it is advisable to maintain a cheerful demeanor. If you are experiencing pain, try to display a reassuring smile. In the event of one's illness, it would be beneficial to maintain a positive demeanor. It has the potential to significantly benefit both your cognitive and physical well-being. When an individual wears a smile, their countenance has the power to elicit reciprocal smiles from the entire world.

Do not succumb to negativity under the false impression that nothing is going well for you; instead, perceive these challenges as tests of character that must be overcome. Maintain a cheerful countenance and consistently display a positive demeanor, as the outcome of circumstances tends to improve when one perseveres in smiling through adversity.

3. Every challenge is accompanied by a corresponding resolution: In circumstances where all indicators suggest a discouraging outcome, it is important to refrain from perceiving oneself as trapped without any viable alternatives. There exists perpetually an avenue of escape, and one can invariably conceive of a resolution to surmount the predicament. Remain calm, engage in deep contemplation, have faith, and witness its manifestation before your very eyes. The resolutions might

manifest as intellectual concepts, they can manifest as individuals or acquaintances capable of providing assistance, they are not limited to familiar persons, and may even emerge through alternative circumstances. If you encounter an impediment that appears insurmountable, endeavor to ascend it; should the obstacle prove too formidable, take measures to dismantle it. There is perpetually an item available to utilize in order to penetrate a barrier...

4. Seek out individuals with a positive outlook and engage in conversations with them: There are instances in which we are unable to tackle a challenge in isolation. In the event that we find ourselves in such circumstances and our determination progressively wanes, it is advisable to seek companionship with individuals who can offer constructive guidance and provide a listening ear devoid of personal judgment. Your

acquaintances or close relatives are the primary individuals to whom you can turn to seek support or assistance. It is imperative to exercise caution when selecting others, as being subject to judgment and criticism is highly undesirable. Optimistic individuals can undeniably present you with a multitude of alternatives to consider. They can unquestionably serve as a sanctuary and means of escape for you.

5. Derive inspiration: Motivation can stem from internal as well as external factors. There exists a considerable array of methods in which you can foster self-motivation. Engage in the consumption of optimistic literature, view uplifting and joyful films, engage in conversations with individuals of a positive disposition, partake in creative endeavors, leisurely engage in activities, and savor delectable cuisine. By fostering the well-being of both your

intellect and physique, you will undoubtedly experience a surge of inspiration. Engage yourself in the reading of quality literature and immerse yourself in narratives that inspire. Draft uplifting and motivational quotes on a notepad, and affix them strategically upon your drawers, refrigerator, or entrance as a constant reminder to maintain an optimistic mindset. It consistently operates without fail.

6. Engage in benevolent actions: Aiding others grants a sense of personal gratification, provoking affirmative sentiments. Assisting others periodically is of great significance as it diverts one's focus from self-centric thoughts. Assist an elderly individual in safely navigating across the road. Provide charitable donations to a child soliciting for aid on a thoroughfare. Babysit your younger sister. Extend an invitation to

collaborate on a project. Extend the use of your umbrella to someone. Donate to charity. Attend to a companion experiencing a difficult situation. Allocate a portion of your time to engage in social interactions. Engage in spontaneous acts of benevolence. Once you have ingrained it as a consistent practice, a positive mindset will manifest effortlessly.

7. Please proceed with the enumeration of the aspects for which you express gratitude. It is imperative to recall the significance attached to cultivating a sense of gratitude, isn't it? Once again, I would like to emphasize that a positive attitude entails expressing gratitude for the things one has been bestowed with. Lack of appreciation for the things you receive will deter others from feeling inclined to offer you their generosity, thereby diminishing the potential joy in giving. Expressing gratitude towards

someone demonstrates your sincere recognition and appreciation for their diligent endeavors and impactful contributions bestowed upon you. Knowing that someone is delighted to receive something from you enhances your own joy in giving further. If one desires to attract an abundance of positive circumstances in life, by exhibiting gratitude, one will be bestowed with increased blessings.

8. Encourage your creativity: In the event of encountering a minor setback, such as feeling overwhelmed by work-related stress, strive to engage in innovative and distinctive activities. Please proceed to your designated recreational area and engage in a game of billiards. Proceed to the fitness center and engage in physical activity. Indulge in a tranquilizing body massage for self-care. Embark on a remarkable journey to a splendid locale and embrace the

fullness of life. Eat something great. Sing, dance and mingle. Divert your attention from your customary habits. This will sever your connection to the negative emotions you experience in your workplace. It will aid in rejuvenating your mental faculties and realigning your focal objectives.

9. Recognize and acknowledge your shortcomings, offer a sincere apology, and proceed forward. It is imperative to acknowledge that perfection is unattainable, as you are considerably distant from it. When one commits an error, it is essential to acknowledge, assume accountability, express remorse, endeavor to rectify it, if feasible, and progress forward. Refrain from fixating on adverse occurrences. It will exacerbate the situation and have a negative impact on your emotional state. Do not allow it to impact you or your interpersonal connections. Advance and

derive a valuable insight from the experience. That is positive attitude.

10. Employ positive language: Instead of utilizing phrases such as "Don't do this" or "You should not do it like this," opt for "It would be preferable if you did it like this" or "Do you believe it would be more beneficial to approach it this way?" Positive language can be challenging to integrate if you are accustomed to expressing ideas negatively. However, it is advisable to commence by refraining from utilizing unfavorable terms such as "do not," "should not," "will not," "would not," and "cannot." When you criticize someone, use a positive tone and don't shout. Commence by presenting a favorable remark, subsequent to which, shift attention towards the shortcomings, elucidating the specifics of the error and providing guidance on rectifying it. If your intention is to engage in rational discourse or address

any concerns, it is advisable to conduct yourself in a reasonable manner. Recognize the actions undertaken by the organization or individual towards you, and articulate your sentiments in a manner conducive to their understanding and acceptance of your rationale.

## How To Strategically Engage With The Opposing Force

Having gained an understanding of the enemy's strengths and methods of attack, we can now strategize and devise various means to overcome the enemy. There are various approaches to addressing cigarette addiction, one of which is commonly referred to as the method of cessation. This approach is most effectively employed when an individual has successfully refrained from smoking for a period exceeding one month, only to encounter an unexpected desire to smoke stemming from exposure to specific triggers associated with smoking. Additionally, this can be put into practice by effortlessly obtaining a package of cigarettes and consuming a single cigarette. Indeed, it is accurate that you would be required to discreetly smoke a single cigarette without detection, effectively evading the attention of those individuals who are aware of your cessation of smoking.

It is crucial to emphasize that you are actively avoiding a relapse into smoking, and instead, you are prioritizing safeguarding yourself against the reestablishment of the habit. Partaking in a single cigarette may be perceived as an act of renunciation of reverting to one's former patterns, as it is crucial to bear in mind our primary objective of avoiding a relapse into habitual smoking.

Non-smokers enjoy a greater amount of time as compared to smokers, as the latter's smoking habit diminishes their available time. A single cigarette typically consumes approximately seven to eleven minutes of time, and smoking an entire pack would add up to a cumulative duration of 140 minutes dedicated solely to smoking. This stark contrast presents itself as a potential occasion to replace those moments of smoking with alternative, non-smoking activities. You would need to devise strategies to utilize those 140 minutes more effectively.

I presumed that you have already established your habitual patterns pertaining to smoking, encompassing the specific timings and locations where you engage in this activity on a daily basis. We have the capacity to substitute these patterns in order to alleviate any sense of emptiness. Consider this scenario: you might find yourself lighting up your initial cigarette shortly after awakening, while enjoying a cup of coffee. If you were to eliminate smoking from your routine, you would need to identify an alternative activity that brings you joy and satisfaction. It has the potential to encompass a wide range of stimuli that provide pleasure or amusement to oneself.

Throughout a span of more than two decades, I have acquired a deep understanding of the proclivities and qualities with which cigarettes assail my well-being. Through various observations, I have attained an understanding of the various manifestations and intentional methods employed by this entity when it launches its attacks. The daily ritual of smoking begins promptly upon awakening - as I sip my coffee, my hand instinctively reaches for a lit cigarette to commence the day. The subsequent cigarette would be succeeded by another, subsequent to the morning meal, and another, and another, until I consume an entire pack of cigarettes.

I have maintained a precise record of the designated time for my smoking activity. One strategy for defeating the adversary is to discern alternative activities to fill the void left by smoking, thereby mitigating the gap. You must establish a structured cigarette regimen and be cognizant of your behavioral and physiological responses during specific instances and activities that trigger the urge to smoke.

The Lucrative Cigarette Industry with Profits Amounting to Billions of Dollars

The tobacco industry is an economically significant sector with an annual revenue in the multi-billion dollar range, and governments worldwide have made incremental progress in phasing out this detrimental product. Nevertheless, it will not completely eradicate individuals who smoke—there will exist new smokers, those who decide to cease smoking, and individuals who opt to persist with the habit.

Cigarettes are fundamentally engineered to foster a cyclical and ingrained pattern of behavior. The discernible consequences of cigarettes are readily apparent. Notwithstanding this fact, individuals persist in patronizing these products due to a certain necessity. Furthermore, the companies responsible for the production of these items demonstrate a profound lack of awareness regarding the detrimental health risks imposed upon the individuals who engage in the consumption of these harmful and toxic substances.

It may be beneficial for us to understand that the primary objective of these large corporations is to drive profit. They essentially show little concern for the target audience of their products, as it is widely known that they purposefully encourage smokers to influence non-smokers through their promotional campaigns. Similarly, individuals who smoke persist in gathering together in clusters. They can be observed engaging in forced respiration at social gatherings.

This is an exceptionally grave issue, whereby we are subjected to deceitful practices from these manufacturers;

consequently, we are being directed into unfamiliar spheres. These companies are failing to assume responsibility for the dangers they pose, thereby jeopardizing our well-being.

It is imperative to recognize the need for empowerment and the pursuit of personal freedom; presently, your circumstances are indicative of a state of enslavement. You are presented with a momentous opportunity to liberate yourself; the attainment of your freedom lies within your reach. It is imperative to acknowledge that the present moment signifies an opportune occasion to cease this detrimental habit. Are you not experiencing fatigue from indulging in smoking and enduring the dissatisfaction caused by corporations that vend these products? You may obtain all that you desire, and cigarettes assuredly do not form a constituent element within it.

Despite the escalating prices of cigarettes and the implementation of numerous anti-smoking initiatives by governments worldwide, smokers persist in their consumption of tobacco products.

It is apparent that smokers are indifferent to the price of cigarettes and will persist in their smoking habit regardless of monetary considerations.

The singular approach to curbing smoking is not merely through educational campaigns and price escalations, but rather by instilling in individuals an awareness that they are being deceived by cigarette manufacturers and the products they offer. Smokers have been ensnared in a cycle of dissatisfaction and deprivation for numerous years, urgently necessitating their emancipation. It is imperative that they embark upon the path to cessation by adhering to the techniques expounded upon within this literary work. The ensuing sections will elucidate the precise steps one should undertake to implement said strategies.

Consider the substantial profits these corporations are generating from consumers like us; it behooves us to ponder whether we truly require these purchases. Have we not been the party experiencing a loss in this transaction? If we persist in maintaining our cigarette consumption, these manufacturers will not only perpetuate harm to ourselves but also to future generations.

The exceptional adaptability inherent to our human nature renders us the most intellectually advanced species on Earth. As a testament to this adaptability, we have the capacity to abstain from smoking, exemplifying our ability to transcend this habit and become non-smokers. If I am capable of achieving it, rest assured that you possess superior abilities and can likewise accomplish the task. Let us commence and cease the act of smoking.

It is imperative that we render cigarette corporations aware of our decision to cease patronizing their products, demonstrating our enhanced consumer discernment and ability to make more informed choices.

Let us collectively unite and partake in the endeavor of sharing our personal odyssey towards a smoke-free existence, with the intention of imparting inspiration upon others to quit smoking. Hence, let us convene to recount our narratives.

## How To Manage Your Cravings

The initial fortnight following the decision to cease smoking tends to be the most tumultuous period in terms of handling the intense desire for cigarettes. Each and every aspect of your being will frequently yearn for a cigarette. This signifies the most arduous phase of smoking cessation, however, there exist several strategies through which you can alleviate cravings and endure this period. Now, let us examine a few of them as presented below.

Prior to commencing the exploration of methods to alleviate the severity of smoking cravings, it is imperative to commence by gaining a comprehensive comprehension of the precise manner in which these cravings manifest.

What are the various categories of cravings?

Culinary desires are classified into two categories. There exists a multitude that persists continuously, revealing itself as a concealed inclination to engage in smoking which perpetually lingers. Despite not being magnified, the sensation persists indefinitely, causing ex-smokers to endure it for an extended duration.

Conversely, there exist fleeting yet vigorous impulses. These urges typically correlate with multiple stimuli, notably stress. Nevertheless, they have a tendency to dissipate within a matter of seconds or minutes. While the frequency of these cravings may decrease over time, it is crucial to bear in mind that their intensity typically remains constant. When endeavoring to mitigate the cravings for cigarette smoking, it is imperative to comprehend the differentiation between these two phenomena and subsequently devise the requisite strategies to effectively mitigate each one.

Approaches for Managing Strong Desires

Whilst cravings are likely to diminish over time, individuals seeking to quit smoking can depend on the subsequent strategies to effectively eliminate these cravings.

## Nicotine Replacement Therapy (NRT)

NRT encompasses a suite of tools meticulously designed to satisfy your body's nicotine cravings while effectively mitigating the presence of harmful components typically found in cigarettes. Nevertheless, the concentration of nicotine in alternate forms, such as vaping devices, is typically reduced compared to that found in cigarettes. Consequently, these alternatives primarily serve to diminish the severity of cravings to more tolerable levels. Certain products utilized as forms of Nicotine Replacement Therapy (NRT) encompass Lozenges, patches, inhalators, as well as mouth and nasal sprays, among various others.

Patches serve primarily to manage underlying cravings as they are designed to gradually release nicotine in small doses over a prolonged duration. Conversely, lozenges and sprays are employed to alleviate sporadic, intense cravings.

Stop Smoking Medicines

There is a wide variety of stop smoking medicines that are suited for use in curbing smoking. These medications are not designed to administer nicotine, but instead function by targeting the brain to alleviate the severity of cravings. Please seek guidance from your healthcare provider for further recommendations regarding the most suitable medication for your condition.

Behavior Change

The conduct exhibited by a smoker differs from that exhibited by a non-smoker. Typically, smokers tend to establish a daily regimen that accommodates their smoking behavior. Therefore, upon making the decision to cease smoking, one must undergo a complete transformation in behavior and embrace a lifestyle that aligns with a new routine. Any items or stimuli that evoke associations with smoking should be removed during the initial weeks when cravings are most intense. This might entail severing ties with friends who smoke and seeking alternative activities to occupy the time previously spent on smoking breaks.

How to Avoid Relapses

Upon cessation of smoking, it is imperative to recognize that maintaining this newfound state will require a continual struggle. While the completion of the withdrawal phase signifies a significant accomplishment in the endeavor to overcome the addiction, there will inevitably be occasions where intense cravings for smoking overpower you, potentially resulting in relapses. Occurrences arise when one, despite having ceased, engages in the act of smoking. It is nevertheless crucial to acknowledge that lapses do not necessitate a return to smoking and subsequently undergoing a complete relapse; they simply indicate the need for greater effort. Given that relapses commonly occur in response to various triggers, it is incumbent upon individuals to identify and proactively avoid these triggers to the best of their ability. Nevertheless, in the event of any unintentional lapse, it is imperative that you do not allow discouragement to set in, but rather maintain your motivation by consistently reminding yourself of the underlying reasons behind your decision to quit.

Utilize the strategies and approaches employed during the withdrawal phase to navigate occasional setbacks and lapses.

Chapter 4:

Motivation

Synopsis

Throughout my experience, I have encountered numerous smokers who, despite lacking the personal desire, exhibited remarkable determination in successfully abstaining from smoking. Occasionally, I come across young individuals who are being compelled by their parents to abstain.

Occasionally, adults find themselves coerced by medical professionals, whereas in other instances, adults are deceived by their relatives and acquaintances who misleadingly entice them to attend educational sessions, disguising them as casual social gatherings, such as dinners. While it would be inappropriate for me to assert that this tactic is universally effective, it is worth noting that it enjoys a higher success rate than what is commonly assumed.

Getting Started

It would be inaccurate to assert that these individuals did not possess any prior inclination or intention to quit smoking. I surmise that a majority of individuals who smoke possess a modicum of inclination to discontinue their habit. However, mere inclination lacks efficacy in the absence of a comprehensive comprehension of nicotine addiction and its corresponding therapeutic measures, thereby rendering it insufficient for achieving success. That is precisely why the majority of seminars endeavor to transmit information as rapidly as feasible.


It is crucial to comprehend the underlying reasons for individuals engaging in smoking, the imperative need for them to discontinue this habit, the strategies and techniques to facilitate cessation, and the methods to maintain long-term freedom from smoking. Each of these four areas constitutes essential aspects for an individual contemplating implementing layoffs. Lacking a thorough understanding of each component, the individual attempting to quit smoking will be hindered in their efforts.


Understanding the rationale behind an individual's smoking habits enables the smoker to recognize that the perceived magical attributes commonly associated with smoking are built upon erroneous beliefs and emotions. Although many smokers believe they smoke out of personal desire, the fundamental reason behind their smoking behavior is actually rooted in dependency. They have developed a dependence and their physiology is demanding the act of smoking. They are individuals with substance abuse issues, without any ambiguity, and recognizing this foundational concept is the pivotal initial step.

Like any other form of addiction or participation in a 12-step program, the acknowledgment of powerlessness over the substance forms the initial stage of the recovery process. It is imperative for you to understand that although you believed that smoking was inducing a sense of calmness, it was actually heightening your levels of tension, or to be more precise, exacerbating your responses to stressful situations.

Despite your belief that smoking can make you feel energetic, the truth is that it is actually depleting your endurance and strength. Smokers frequently perceive smoking as a means to derive enjoyment and foster a more socially engaged lifestyle-

Styles, it is undoubtedly impeding and constraining your ability to participate in a myriad of activities and forge new acquaintances.

Instead of fostering a vibrant and engaged role within society, it is actually encouraging you to engage in a multitude of antisocial behaviors.

It prompted you to engage in smoking during social interactions, frequently resulting in your absence from gatherings or your decision to decline attending events where smoking is prohibited. The information regarding the imperative need for an individual to cease the habit of smoking is arguably of the least astonishing nature, as it is widely acknowledged among numerous smokers that engaging in this detrimental practice poses severe health risks.

The matter at hand revolves around the lack of awareness amongst the majority regarding the severity of the situation. Numerous individuals find themselves greatly overwhelmed upon fully grasping the substantial extent of the hazards associated with smoking.

The recognition that ceasing smoking is indeed a struggle for survival holds significant prominence in achieving sustained success. This information is frequently crucial for addressing the intermittent thoughts that continue to be triggered by conditions and situations encountered over the course of the former smoker's life.

How to quit - indeed, this revelation comes as a surprise to many: individuals initially discontinue the habit upon realizing that smoking is detrimental to their health. They then discover that the huge majority of these people quit cold turkey.

I have witnessed the profound impact of education in facilitating the successful cessation of smoking in countless instances.

Once more, that matter encompasses more than merely elucidating the physical dangers associated with smoking. "It implies that the individual who smokes acquires a comprehensive understanding of the tangible aspects,

The cognitive, societal, financial, and artistic implications of smoking. In addition, I have observed how personal comprehension has evolved into a formidable instrument employed by thousands of former smokers to maintain their determination to abstain from cigarettes.

They will uphold their determination as long as they continue to appreciate the underlying reasons for their decision to quit, and consistently prioritize those motivations in their consciousness.

Could we potentially inspire a smoker to desire quitting? Many individuals who have been smoking cigarettes for a considerable duration already possess a strong level of motivation.

While it is possible that not all smokers in general share this characteristic, it is probable that any individual smoker who voluntarily visits a quit smoking clinic or conducts an online search using the keywords "stop smoking" possesses a degree of initial apprehension and seeks further guidance regarding the process of quitting.

In essence, the response to the question of whether an individual may have the inclination to quit is affirmative. In fact, it can be observed that a majority of smokers already possess a degree of motivation in this regard. Understand the significance of ceasing tobacco consumption, maintaining abstinence from smoking, and safeguarding your well-being.

"Just one more..."

NO. Wrong mentality. The notion of "an additional one" or "a final one" is detrimental. Upon making the decision to cease, it is imperative that one does not indulge in a final act of smoking for the sake of celebration. It is emotionally daunting to relinquish reliance on anything. In the event that one relies on their partner, the loss of that individual can be significant, regardless of the detrimental nature of the relationship. The dependency formed creates a sense of disorientation and emptiness upon their absence. It adheres to a similar premise in regard to smoking. You will come to apprehend that you formerly engaged solely with a specific set of individuals during designated periods for smoking, or that your visits to the nearest gasoline station for the purpose of tobacco acquisition have become infrequent.

Remove any smoking-related stimuli, such as lighters and old cigarette boxes, from your field of vision. Indeed, throughout one's existence, encounters with individuals who intentionally expose one to genuine smoke, thereby evoking strong emotional responses, may arise, ultimately igniting a desire for a cigarette. Ensuring that you reside in a secure environment free from tobacco smoke during the initial days of quitting smoking is crucial. Disposing of an ash tray, for example, also demonstrates one's dedication to their goals.

Eliminate Traces of Smoking

There is a multitude of reminders pertaining to the act of smoking, which frequently elicit a strong response, enabling one to rationalize their smoking behavior. It is imperative to promptly dispose of cigarettes, either by discarding them or selling them to another individual. However, it is crucial to remove them from your possession. Do not conceal them in your secure storage or any such place; instead, eliminate the most significant allure by parting with them.

Task: Compose an inventory enumerating all the prompts or cues associated with smoking that are present in your daily existence. From a receptacle for discarded cigarette ash to an individual engaging in the act of smoking in a public area. To obtain additional scoring, assign numerical values ranging from 1 to 10 based on the extent to which they elicit a reaction from you. Afterwards, proceed to remove the items within your capability to do so (for example, the ashtray, not the individual smoking outdoors).

Assignment: Replicate the aforementioned process for each of your triggers, ensuring the inclusion of emotional triggers such as conflicts with one's spouse.

Excellent job! It can be quite challenging to identify one's triggers and ascertain how they exert an emotional influence, thereby exerting a degree of control over one's behavior.

First days

Approach each day with a granular mindset, even down to the minute if necessary. It's not easy. However, it is possible to proactively identify potential triggers and develop coping strategies.

First, identify the triggers. Some examples of these could involve the presence of an ashtray, a gas station (from which one commonly acquires cigarettes), or...

Adhering to a smoke-free lifestyle

Preserving a lifestyle free from tobacco smoke poses numerous challenges. It is imperative to sustain one's motivation. You can do this. There are compelling justifications for abstaining from smoking.

What if you relapse?

In the event of a relapse, it should be noted that it does not signify the ultimate demise or catastrophic outcome. Although it is suboptimal, it should not serve as a justification to abandon your aspirations of quitting smoking. If you relapsed, go back to your relevant journal entries and remind yourself that it's okay. Please review the correspondence you composed for situations of this nature. Reiterate the justifications for refraining from smoking to yourself. And out of all the progress you have accomplished.

Relapse Assignment:

Please provide a comprehensive account outlining the sequence of events that culminated in the occurrence of the event (smoking/relapse). At every juncture within the process, it is imperative for one to discern and acknowledge the corresponding affective states in the following manner: "

"Observed a blemish on the vehicle" (emotion: displeasure, irritation, concern)

I regretfully arrived tardy to my workplace, eliciting feelings of frustration, embarrassment, concern, disappointment, and apprehension.

It is important to provide an exhaustive account of events, exchanges, and emotions in your list, as this will greatly enhance the overall impact. The objective is to carefully examine your chain of events and discern any factors that may have precipitated, accrued, or had a hand in the relapse. Afterwards, you may analyze the actions that could have been undertaken at each of those junctures to alter the resultant situation. This particular insight was acquired through my study of Dialectical Behavior Therapy (DBT).

Exercise self-compassion while maintaining personal responsibility. Please revisit your previous journal assignments and acknowledge the considerable effort you have exerted thus far. Extract knowledge and insight from instances of relapse and errors, and persist in your endeavors with unwavering determination!

Cancer

It is estimated that tobacco usage is responsible for approximately 33% of global mortality. In excess of sixty distinct carcinogenic substances have been detected within the composition of cigarette smoke, comprising nitrosamines that are exclusively found in tobacco and polycyclic aromatic hydrocarbons.

Within the human body, enzymes are present with the specific purpose of metabolizing and eliminating carcinogens. However, on certain occasions, their functionality may be compromised, leading to the attachment of carcinogens to DNA within cells, thereby resulting in detrimental consequences. Tumors develop as a result of the proliferation and accumulation of abnormal DNA-containing cells that are capable of survival and reproduction. Malignant cells have the ability to undergo metastasis, thereby disseminating and infiltrating distant anatomical sites within the body. The intrinsic toxicity of tobacco contributes to the risk of developing cancer; however, the intensity and duration of exposure are also influential factors.

The correlation between the length and regularity of smoking and the heightened susceptibility to cancer brought about by tobacco consumption is evident. As a result, addiction promotes persistent and extensive contact with carcinogens, thereby serving as a formidable indirect catalyst for various ailments.

Given the fact that a large percentage of cigarette smokers are heavy smokers who directly inhale nicotine into their lungs, it is not surprising that active smoking and exposure to ambient tobacco smoke are believed to be responsible for approximately 90% of all cases of lung cancer.

In all nations where smoking rates have increased, there has been a drastic surge in the occurrence of lung cancer. Lung cancer stands as the primary contributor to fatalities caused by cancer in the United States, claiming the lives of both males and females at distressing levels.

If smoking cessation were universally achieved today, it is estimated that approximately 80% of occurrences of lung cancer would be preempted. Nevertheless, it should be noted that the respiratory system is not the sole susceptibility of carcinogenic agents. The correlation between cigarette smoking and the development of laryngeal, oral, and esophageal cancers, as well as bladder and pancreatic cancers, is significant.

The likelihood of cancer occurrence diminishes markedly when a chronic tobacco user ultimately eradicates the addiction. On the other hand, individuals who engage in the use of smokeless tobacco experience a markedly elevated probability of developing malignancies of the head and neck region, primarily attributed to the repetitive exposure of the oral mucosa to harmful toxins.

In comparison to American smokeless tobacco, the utilization of Swedish smokeless tobacco ("snus") seems to be associated with a lower incidence of tobacco-related cancer.

The prevalence of oral tobacco consumption exhibits significant variations across different regions, with a higher incidence observed in certain parts of the United States, Sweden, India, and Southeast Asia.

Pulmonary illness

It is not surprising that individuals who smoke cigarettes are prone to a wide range of respiratory diseases in addition to lung cancer. Chronic obstructive pulmonary disease (COPD) is a prominent medical condition that stands as a significant contributor to the incapacitation and death rates among individuals who engage in cigarette smoking.

The prevalence of COPD is seen in over 80% of individuals who engage in smoking, and a high incidence of premature mortality is observed among those afflicted with this ailment. Chronic obstructive pulmonary disease (COPD) is the term used to encompass diseases affecting the respiratory system that lead to obstruction of airflow. It seems that the airways in females are particularly affected by the impact of cigarette smoke.

Dyspnea is frequently observed in females diagnosed with chronic obstructive pulmonary disease (COPD), whereas females experience a higher prevalence of airway wall thickening compared to males. Whilst diagnostic criteria may differ, chronic obstructive pulmonary disease (COPD) frequently encompasses the presence of chronic bronchitis (marked by a persistent cough and phlegm production) as well as emphysema (characterized by prolonged expansion of air spaces and degeneration of lung wall tissue).

The rise in the incidence of multiple respiratory afflictions, such as pneumonia, the common cold, and influenza, may likewise be ascribed to the practice of active smoking and the exposure to ambient tobacco smoke.

Should a smoker acquire any of these diseases, their recovery time would be substantially lengthened in comparison to that of a non-smoker. The presence of secondhand smoke significantly exacerbates the adverse effects on the well-being of children. Children face an elevated susceptibility to the development of asthma and chronic cough when they are raised in an environment where smoking is prevalent, consequently leading to a potential impairment of their respiratory growth and functionality.

Coronary illness

For a considerable duration, it has been well-established that the act of smoking cigarettes significantly elevates the risk of developing cardiovascular disease. As previously stated, the carbon monoxide present in cigarette smoke forms a bond with hemoglobin within the bloodstream, resulting in a decrease in the availability of molecules that carry oxygen. As a result, the heart necessitates exerting greater effort in order to supply the body with the essential oxygen it requires.

The occurrence of myocardial infarction, heart attack, and stroke is significantly higher among smokers due to the induced physiological stress. Nevertheless, the incidence of smoking-related cardiovascular disease exhibits considerable variability depending on geographical location and gender. Tobacco consumption is a major contributing factor to approximately 30 to 40 percent of all fatalities observed in both the United States and Europe. However, in China, where the prevalence of tobacco use among adult males is alarmingly high at over 53 percent (in contrast to a mere 2.4 percent among adult females), the proportion of smoking-related deaths attributable to cardiovascular disease is notably lower.

Moreover, research indicates that women who indulge in smoking, even to a moderate extent (between 1 and 14 cigarettes per day), experience a substantial rise in the likelihood of sudden cardiac death. Reductions in the risk for cardiovascular disease become evident within a year of smoking cessation, while the decline in risk for lung cancer requires more time to manifest subsequent to quitting smoking.

reduction in the organism's capacity to deliver sufficient oxygen to crucial organs and muscles (heightening susceptibility to conditions like coronary artery disease, peripheral artery disease, and diabetes).

Childhood diseases, such as the common cold, exhibit a higher incidence in households where adults engage in the act of smoking.

## Allow Us To Collaborate In Discovering Your Fundamental Purpose.

We have extensively discussed various motivations behind individuals' desire to cease their activities, as well as the multifaceted advantages that may ensue. However, I kindly request that you provide additional precision and detail in your response. If you are able to provide precise details regarding your motivation, it will enable you to firmly grasp onto it.

"I want to stay healthy," is not nearly as effective as, "I don't want to die from emphysema like my uncle did," or, "I don't want to have to sleep with a COPD machine over my face every night looking like Darth Vader so that my son is afraid of me at night and doesn't want to sleep in the same room as me."

The fundamental reason behind my decision was that I did not wish to depart from this world before my time and leave my daughter to face it alone.

Preserving every moment with her is of utmost significance to me. Hence, despite my current location on this dock, where I am dictating this book, it holds great importance that she remains within my line of sight, merely fifty yards away, engaged in training with our kickboxing instructor. That is the level of significance my personal purpose holds.

There are numerous reasons that can establish a connection with you. I propose the following alternative phrasing in a formal tone: "Consider the possibility of reallocating the funds attributed to my annual tobacco expenditure towards the acquisition of a new vehicle or an indulgent travel experience, thus designating a specific goal for saving instead."

Reflection Questions

Examine each distinct set of advantages associated with abstaining from smoking and determine which ones align with your personal preferences to the greatest extent.

After identifying the categories that strongly resonate with your interests, proceed to arrange them in order of duration and emotional attachment for effective organization.

Construct precise assertions regarding each of these classifications, such as, "I harbour no desire to meet an untimely demise," or, "I hold trepidation pertaining to the possibility of developing lung carcinoma," or, "It is my fervent wish that my progeny never gaze into my eyes and inquire about my mortality."

Proceed with this procedure, addressing these inquiries until you ascertain your underlying motivation. It will be the answer that affects you most deeply, the one that feels visceral; it will hit you in the stomach and make you want to cry as you're writing it down. That is the moment in which you have discovered the purpose behind your actions.

Your Action Plan

Continue to work through these reflection questions and dial in to finding your ultimate why. As an integral aspect of this undertaking, we invite you to contemplate becoming a member of a community or our esteemed Facebook group, where you can actively engage by sharing inquiries pertaining to your unique encounters. It is not necessary for you to engage in this process in seclusion; therefore, your task is to locate and join a community and share your reason for participating.

If you have yet to establish a clear purpose or reason behind your actions, you may avail yourself of the opportunity to inquire within the group, peruse the motivations of others, and harness the support of this community to ascertain your own. After disseminating the information among our community, make sure to record it in your journal and incorporate it into your vision board.

Jot down your objective and render it perceptible. Translate your thoughts from the realm of imagination and project them onto tangible reality. After establishing a connection with our community and crafting a compelling visualization, proceed to Step 2 and accompany me in the subsequent chapter.

Chapter Four: Making Preparations for Departure

Cessation of smoking cannot be achieved instantaneously. A primary factor contributing to individuals' inability to abandon the habit is their propensity to underestimate the complex nature of overcoming it. There are individuals who hold the belief that accomplishing this task can be achieved expeditiously, however, such an approach often results in discontentment in the event that circumstances do not unfold as anticipated. Cessation of smoking requires dedication, self-discipline, and a resolute commitment to employing any necessary means. In order to enhance your prospects, it is imperative that you demonstrate complete readiness to adopt a smoke-free way of life. This chapter will present a set of recommendations to aid individuals in adequately preparing themselves for smoking cessation.

Consider the pros and cons of quitting - The advantages of quitting smoking are surely lengthy. Nevertheless, there are also benefits to be gained from abstaining from smoking. On which side of the fence do you position yourself? Please deliberate on compiling a thorough list of the advantages and disadvantages associated with permanently ceasing your tobacco consumption. When contemplating this matter subsequent to its completion, it is imperative to evaluate whether the positive aspects supersede the negative ones, or conversely. Your response to this question will serve as an indicator of your readiness to cease smoking. If you express that the benefits of quitting smoking outweigh the challenges, it would effectively enhance your level of motivation.

Take into account the challenges you will face - As previously stated, ceasing the habit of smoking will undoubtedly be a formidable endeavor. What leads you to believe that the act of resigning would present certain difficulties? Create a comprehensive inventory detailing the factors that contribute to the formidable nature of relinquishing the habit of tobacco use, even if only in a hypothetical context. This measure will equip you for the imminent challenges you are to encounter upon embarking on your quest to cease. In addition to offering additional incentive, it will provide you with a preview of the challenges that lie ahead. Equally significant is that it promotes a proactive approach towards addressing these issues, prompting individuals to contemplate potential remedies well in advance.

Reflect upon the motivations for cessation - Each individual possesses their own rationale for relinquishing smoking. Certain individuals engage in such behavior due to the presence of preexisting health conditions. Other individuals engage in this behavior due to apprehension surrounding the potential acquisition of illnesses in the future. There are individuals who engage in this activity due to fiscal considerations. People engage in such behavior as a deterrent for others to imitate their actions. Regardless of the motivations driving you, it is imperative that you consistently recall and reinforce them. Please bear in mind that these considerations may prove instrumental in your ability to navigate the challenging circumstances that lie ahead. Devise alternatives to smoking - Another contributing factor to the failure of many individuals in their quitting journey arises from the oversight of exploring cessation methods. It is imperative to consider alternative strategies to successfully mitigate the cravings, particularly in the case of long-term smokers who have developed a habitual inclination to engage in smoking. There exist numerous strategies to overcome cravings, with certain techniques exhibiting greater efficacy depending on the individual. Some of the most widely employed strategies for combating smoking cravings encompass engaging in physical activities such as walking, hydrating oneself by drinking water, executing spontaneous movements, or seeking restful sleep.

Set a date for quitting - Setting a date goes beyond creating a formality for your quitting. It would be necessary to establish a specific date on which you intend to engage in the activity, thereby affording yourself adequate time to sufficiently prepare oneself both physically and mentally for the forthcoming endeavor. Upon the arrival of the specified date, it is imperative that you adhere to your commitment and employ every possible effort to cease smoking. Please dispose of any cigarette-related materials by the specified date and resist the urge to purchase them, even in the face of temptation. In order to achieve optimal outcomes, it is imperative to embark upon a transitional journey encompassing the reduction of consumption, the mitigation of cravings, and ultimately, the cessation of tobacco purchases.

Ceasing tobacco use is an arduous undertaking, thus it is imperative to maintain both physical and mental readiness for the challenges that lie ahead. Adhere to these recommendations to enhance your chances of successfully transitioning and overcoming the habit.

## 3
## Cease the Habit of Smoking Permanently Through Utilization of Subliminal Hypnosis Techniques!

H
ypnosis
to stop
The smoker demonstrates notable efficiency and longevity when utilized correctly. If you have attempted and failed with nearly every alternative approach, it may be appropriate to consider engaging in a course of smoking cessation therapy utilizing hypnotherapy, which offers a promising and enduring solution to permanently break free from this deleterious

addiction. With the aid of hypnosis, quitting smoking can be achieved in a natural manner. In the event that you have previously explored numerous methodologies to combat smoking, perhaps it is the opportune occasion to avail yourself of the benefits provided by hypnotherapy, as its proper implementation can unconditionally aid you in achieving your goal of quitting smoking. There is a significant number of individuals who both smoke and desire to quit smoking permanently, however, overcoming this addiction has proven to be incredibly challenging. Recently, numerous innovative techniques for self-improvement have emerged, aiming to facilitate smoking cessation and assist individuals in their weight loss efforts.

The analgesic, which has effectively alleviated discomfort for numerous individuals, is now poised to provide assistance to you. The effectiveness of this approach to quit smoking lies in its ability to cultivate one's cognition, which inherently serves as the most crucial avenue for breaking any form of behavioral patterns. Renounce any form of addiction, including smoking, through the utilization of Subliminal Hypnosis. Presently, there exist numerous deliberations concerning the use of this technique for altering the mind and enhancing personal growth. It is now widely acknowledged as a straightforward and organic approach to achieving profound and enduring transformation.

Analgesic has increasingly gained recognition as a widely accepted method through which individuals can gain access to the depths of their subconscious and, effectively, reshape their limited and pessimistic beliefs. It is a powerful tool that enables one to eradicate these negative qualities and undergo transformative change. This is the reason why employing analgesic as a means to aid smokers in quitting their addiction is considered a rapid and readily available solution when compared to the utilization of nicotine patches, chewing gum, and expensive prescribed medical treatments. Cease tobacco use through the administration of an analgesic for a comprehensive and conclusive evaluation.

Preliminary analysts: Discern the underlying incentives

Motivation is essential for any smoker who wants to quit. Hence, it is of utmost significance to employ techniques that enhance the patient's motivation in smoking cessation interventions.

Regarding the operator:

The operator is required to exhibit a genuine curiosity in comprehending the patient's situation. In order to render this interest tangible, it is advisable to engage in contemplation and consolidation of the patient's statements during the interview.
The operator is required to assist the patient, while considering their

objectives and principles, in cultivating an understanding of the disparity between their current circumstances and desired future state. Having a profound understanding of the substantial disparities between our current state and our desired state is imperative when seeking to initiate potential modifications in our behavior.

The resistance exhibited by patients should be acknowledged and regarded as a natural indication of their apprehension and uncertainties surrounding the process of change. If the operator engages in confrontational or argumentative behavior towards the patient, it elicits an increase in the patient's resistance. It is advantageous to strategically navigate resistance and proactively mitigate conflict situations during the interview.

The operator fosters the patient's self-esteem by demonstrating belief in his capabilities to bring about change and conveying gratitude for the endeavors undertaken during the cessation procedures.

Regarding the patient, the discussion becomes somewhat more intricate. There are numerous inquiries that individuals who choose to cease smoking frequently pose to themselves.

The correlation between smoking and health outcomes is indeed robust, intricate, and deeply intertwined. Reaching the conclusion to terminate a relationship can be challenging since there are instances where individuals are reluctant to let go, despite recognizing that such relationships are detrimental rather than beneficial. To successfully embrace a smoke-free lifestyle permanently, it is imperative to conquer the psychological snares that persuade us into perceiving the pleasure derived from each cigarette outweighs the associated dangers. It is crucial to acknowledge that the hazards of smoking are not inconcrete figures, but rather, these statistics hold direct implications for each individual who smokes. You must devote effort towards cultivating your self-esteem and persuading yourself of your capability to accomplish it. Simultaneously, it is imperative that you dispel any apprehension or feelings of embarrassment when it comes to seeking assistance.

Patient Question and Answer Session for Motivational Discovery

I am consciously decreasing the quantity of cigarettes consumed. Why is there a necessity to cease?

It is true that quantitycan makea difference, in terms of health risks, and that the less you smoke thebetter,the more true it is that no cigarette is risk-free.
Clinical evidence indicates that the act of smoking, even on as few as five occasions per month, can result in the onset of coughing and a sensation of breathlessness. Furthermore, the consumption of fewer than four

cigarettes per day has been found to elevate the likelihood of mortality arising from heart attacks and other related ailments. Despite the relatively low number of cigarettes consumed, the probability of developing cancer and respiratory ailments remains above average. Similar to the consumption of cigarettes, including even a small quantity, the susceptibility of women to developing lung cancer appears to be higher than that of men.

Hence, even individuals who engage in smoking to such a minimal extent that they may be reluctant to identify themselves as regular smokers, there exists a compelling rationale to cease the habit entirely. Considering the presence of an additional factor: in comparison to heavy smokers, individuals who smoke in lesser quantities exhibit a diminished level of nicotine dependence, consequently leading to a more feasible prospect of breaking the addiction.

Smoking serves as a coping mechanism for alleviating stress. I do not believe I can manage without it.

One of the prominent fallacies associated with smoking is the erroneous belief that cigarettes serve as an effective means of stress management. Indeed, the root cause of stress and anxiety stems from the longing to smoke, which is subsequently alleviated upon smoking a cigarette, thus perpetuating a relentless cycle.

The underlying factors contributing to this phenomenon can be attributed to nicotine, a potent substance known to induce addictive behaviors. Nicotine affects a wide range of mechanisms within the brain, serving to elicit the release of dopamine, a substance known for its ability to generate sensations of positive affect. In individuals who smoke, cigarettes serve as a catalyst for the generation and secretion of these compounds, consequently leading to an increase in addiction as the desire to experience its effects intensifies. The existence of these mechanisms consequently gives rise to the compulsion to smoke, which, for the smoker, manifests as a state of perpetual tension that can only be alleviated when they engage in the act of lighting a cigarette. Nonetheless, this advantage is only transitory since as the level of concentration in the body diminishes, the mechanism is once more triggered, leading to a resurgence in stress levels.

Hence, it can be observed that individuals who smoke tend to exhibit elevated levels of stress in comparison to their non-smoking counterparts, as evidenced by the average data. The positive development is that after a period of three months refraining from smoking, the body no longer requires the stimulus of nicotine, ultimately allowing the body to regain control over these mechanisms and revert back to a state of normalcy.

I have been engaging in smoking for a significant number of years. What is the rationale behind ceasing one's efforts at this juncture?

Indeed, it is a veritable fact: whereby the lengthier one's history of smoking, the greater the extent of bodily harm already inflicted by the consumption of cigarettes. Nonetheless, it is crucial to bear in mind that irrespective of one's age (even after prolonged years of smoking), it is always advantageous to cease the habit.

Abstaining from smoking has both enduring and immediate repercussions.

A individual who ceased their smoking habit at the age of 50 significantly reduces their likelihood of mortality within the subsequent 15 years by 50%. At the age of 65, his mortality risk is equivalent to that of individuals who have never engaged in smoking. Furthermore, it should be noted that even in advanced stages of life, ceasing tobacco use significantly diminishes the likelihood of developing cardiovascular disease and various types of malignancies. In general, individuals who have advanced in age and possess extensive exposure to cigarettes would find it advantageous to cease smoking due to the immediate benefits associated with it. Specifically, the enhancement of blood circulation, respiratory capacity, and the consequent surge in energy levels would significantly contribute to an enhanced quality of life. This is particularly crucial given that any physical limitations encountered at this stage of life could hasten the decline of self-sufficiency.

I have previously ceased smoking and successfully restored my well-being on each occasion. Is it prudent to attempt it once more?

Sure. Utilizing prior experience can prove invaluable in achieving resolute cessation from the habit, once and for all. Prior to attempting to quit smoking once more, it is advisable to develop a systematic approach and, above all, thoroughly assess the reasons behind your past failures to attain this objective.

Gaining comprehension of the factors that contributed to the reinitiation of smoking could serve as the initial stride towards permanently renouncing the habit of tobacco consumption.

I am persuading myself to believe that it would be advantageous to cease smoking. However, I am currently seeking a favorable opportunity to undertake this task.

Many smokers commonly seek circumstances or reasons that provide motivation for them to cease smoking. Take a moment to consider, and you will soon realize that life is replete with abundant opportunities.

For instance, on the commencement of the year. Which individuals do not formulate effective New Year's resolutions? Commencing the year by parting ways with the detrimental habit of smoking is indeed one of the most splendid gifts you can bestow upon yourself. Additionally, it offers convenience by simply referring to the calendar to keep track of the elapsed days, weeks, and months since you stopped smoking cigarettes.

Alternatively, as the arrival of spring draws near, numerous individuals begin contemplating their pursuit of physical fitness in preparation for the summer season. Incorporating a more nutritious diet and establishing a consistent exercise routine seamlessly aligns with the decision to cease tobacco consumption. It will experience a restoration of its overall well-being, as well as a marked improvement in its aesthetic appearance. Smoking, to be precise, diminishes the vitality and radiance of the skin. Additionally, it gives the impression of fatigue and a lack of vitality.

Ceasing smoking before the arrival of springtime can yield significant benefits for individuals afflicted with allergies, as the intensity of their symptoms tends to peak during this season and is further exacerbated by tobacco use.

During the summer months, one can seize the occasion of the commencement of the vacation period or engage in mountain excursions or coastal swimming endeavors that would be less arduous if one refrains from the habit of smoking. In perusing the calendar, one would find an abundance of valid justifications for partaking in smoking, regardless of the month at hand.

In addition to the aforementioned significant life events. When one desires to conceive a child, as smoking has an impact on fertility, or upon assuming the role of a parent or grandparent, an additional incentive to quit can be safeguarding the child from second-hand smoke, or merely the aspiration to enhance the likelihood of witnessing their growth for an extended period of time. Alternatively, in the context of career transitions, various research studies indicate that supervisors generally hold a more favorable perception of individuals who refrain from engaging in tobacco consumption. There is no shortage of opportunities; therefore, it is imperative to seize them, or alternatively, to proactively seek them out.

I would prefer to cease, however, the timing is inappropriate.

Indeed, it holds true that certain occasions may be less conducive to the act of smoking cessation. During particularly challenging periods, attempting to quit smoking may result in unintended consequences. It becomes possible that one may lack the necessary willpower to abstain from smoking, thus undermining their motivation to quit altogether.

Therefore, it is advisable to carefully consider the appropriate moment to participate, by evaluating whether there are specific external circumstances during that period that may impact its favorable outcome. The crucial aspect lies in ensuring that the quest for an opportune occasion does not function as a justification for delay, and that once the determination to conclude is reached, it is steadfastly pursued until completion.

I am interested in resigning; however, it appears that I am unable to do so. I'm too addicted.

Overcoming nicotine addiction is a considerable challenge, particularly for individuals who have been smoking persistently and with greater intensity over an extended period of time. There is unquestionably no doubt about that, however, one should consider the fact that each year, tens of thousands of individuals successfully quit smoking, thereby acknowledging the possibility of achieving such a feat.

You need to have a good deal of determination, and the ideal is to get help from a professional.

Not succumbing to trepidation regarding failure and acknowledging one's dependency is not morally reprehensible nor indicative of frailty. Contrarily, it signifies an initial stride towards gaining a realistic understanding of your affiliation with smoking and readying yourself for the unavoidable manifestations of withdrawal, such as agitation, exhaustion, and diminished focus.

I have made the decision to discontinue my smoking habit. However, I have no desire to experience weight gain.

Indeed, it is a fact that the vast majority of individuals who cease smoking tend to experience an increase in body weight. Nevertheless, it is crucial to recognize that there is no mechanism of automation involved in this process. The extent to which weight gain occurs is primarily determined by one's post-smoking behavior rather than the direct effects of smoking.

Typically, individuals who cease the habit of smoking experience an increase in body weight ranging from approximately 4 to 5 kilograms during the initial weeks. Approximately 30 percent of this augmentation (averaging at 1.5 kg) can be attributed to the eradication of the cigarette's immediate impact on the bodily functions, particularly its influence on basal metabolism resulting in heightened calorie consumption. The lingering weight gain can be attributed to an increased appetite sensation. Frequently, a significant portion of this weight gain can be attributed to snacks consumed outside of regular meal times, which serve as a substitute for cigarettes and are accompanied by similar habitual movements. In numerous instances, consequently, opting for low-calorie foods (such as fruits and vegetables) for daily snacks can effectively minimize the surplus calorie consumption and, thereby, mitigate weight gain. If you were to seize the opportunity to engage in regular physical exercise (consisting of a thirty-minute daily regimen of sustained walking), you could potentially circumvent weight gain altogether, or potentially curtail its incidence to a greater extent.

Nevertheless, notwithstanding the absence of these precautions, various studies indicate that the additional weight gained during the smoking cessation phase is often shed within the first year among individuals who do not smoke. Hence, it is advisable to direct your attention towards achieving your objective, while bearing in mind that shedding those few kilograms shall be accomplished with composure, and that the merits of quitting smoking far surpass the detriments associated with potential weight gain.

I've decided to quit. What are the chances of me succeeding?

It is important to acknowledge from the outset that ceasing the habit of smoking is a challenging endeavor, with a significant likelihood of encountering setbacks and difficulties. Nicotine dependency is highly potent and discontinuing its consumption can elicit symptoms that, particularly during the initial few days, can significantly influence one's daily routine. Furthermore, even after the symptoms subside, the tendency to engage in smoking may resurface. The probabilities of achieving this objective exhibit considerable divergence among individuals. Nonetheless, three primary factors appear to exert a more substantial influence on the likelihood of attaining success.

What is the duration of smoking?

the daily quantity of cigarettes consumed;

The magnitude of withdrawal symptoms experienced during cessation attempts.

On the whole, it appears that women exhibit a higher propensity for failure. The underlying causes need further clarification, but it is probable that women face greater complexities when overcoming addiction due to psychological and physiological factors. Renouncing a societal demeanor and gestures proves to be more challenging, as the repercussions on mood and societal pressures are greatly feared.

## Quit Smoking Benefit

Ceasing tobacco use can be quite challenging; nevertheless, it is within your capabilities. When you renounce smoking, the benefits commence within minutes of your last cigarette. A few noteworthy outcomes of quitting smoking.

Smoking has detrimental effects on one's overall well-being. Smoking detrimentally affects various systems and organs within the human body. Smoking is a practice where a substance, typically tobacco, is combusted and the resulting smoke is either tasted or inhaled.

Smoking not only poses a detrimental impact on your health but also impairs the well-being of those in your vicinity. Enduring exposure to secondhand smoke, commonly known as environmental tobacco smoke or passive smoking, encompasses both exhaled smoke and the emissions from combusted cigarettes. Cigarette smoking is responsible for 87 percent of fatalities caused by lung cancer.

It also holds responsibility for numerous other malignancies and health complications. These conditions encompass respiratory illness, cardiovascular conditions, cerebrovascular events, and ocular disorders. Females who engage in smoking are at a higher risk of experiencing certain fertility complications or the unfortunate event of infant mortality due to sudden infant death syndrome (SIDS).

Smoking is widely acknowledged as a prevalent form of recreational drug consumption. Currently, tobacco smoking stands as the most widely acknowledged form of smoking. Nicotine is a naturally occurring organic compound found in tobacco.

It has a highly addictive nature comparable to that of heroin or cocaine. Over the course of time, an individual progressively develops a physical and emotional dependence on, or becomes subjugated by, nicotine. You will perceive that you are capable of accomplishing challenging tasks and exerting greater control over your life.

Embracing abandonment facilitates self-acceptance. The cessation of smoking brings about notable and tangible health advantages for individuals of both genders and various age groups. Compensation is provided to individuals with and without smoking-related illnesses.

The incidence of developing cardiovascular discomfort resulting from smoking could potentially be reduced by up to fifty percent within a period of one to two years after cessation. Females who discontinue smoking prior to conception or within the initial trimester of pregnancy can significantly diminish their likelihood of giving birth to an underweight infant to levels comparable with those of non-smoking individuals. The health benefits associated with ceasing smoking surpass any potential risks involving minimal weight gain and any subsequent emotional or psychological issues resulting from quitting.

Females who relinquish their pursuits by the age of 35 limit their occupational presumption by a span of 6 to 8 years. There is always room for acquiring benefits from resigning. When an individual chooses to give up smoking, the period of 3 to 9 months following the abdication is characterized by the progression of coughing, asthmatic symptoms, and difficulties in breathing, as the lung functions are augmented by as much as 10%.

The act of being forsaken at the age of 45 culminates in an approximate extension of occupational engagement by a duration of 6 to 7 years. The act of being left or forsaken at the age of 55 results in an extension of active engagement by a period ranging from 3 to 6 years. The act of being left or abandoned at the age of 65 results in an increase in the estimated number of active years by a range of 1.4 to 4 years.

## Embrace The Impetus To Cease Smoking

It is widely acknowledged among smokers that smoking is frequently perceived as pleasurable. You believe that cigarettes provide companionship, solace, and pleasure. One can concurrently associate ceasing smoking with notions of hardship, grief, and self-denial. The subliminal reinforcement of these conflicting emotions transpires in the backdrop of your cognition. Consequently, you may harbor unconstructive and erroneous beliefs that merely reflect your distorted perceptions of actuality. Utilize these recommendations to facilitate the detection of negative thoughts and effectively recondition your mindset towards positive thinking in the process of overcoming your nicotine dependency.

Engaging in tobacco use while also ensuring sufficient sleep at night requires an individual prone to self-destructive behavior. If you persist in engaging in those outdated mental manipulations, be prepared to undergo an arduous and trying period of self-reflection and redemption. Therefore, I urge you to opt for the uncomplicated path ahead. Alter your viewpoint and engage in innovative, enjoyable cognitive exercises.

Do not resign solely due to necessity. Rather, embark on the arduous yet gratifying journey of self-teaching to overcome the habit of smoking. The second option is comparatively more convenient and pleasurable.

It should be acknowledged that it will require effort on your part, although it is advisable to wholeheartedly engage in the process rather than oppose it. To initiate your process, contemplate the subsequent cognitive activities:

I strongly advise against succumbing to the notion of "I must indulge in smoking." Such sentiments are excessively sentimental. Alter it to a statement of greater formality, such as "Please rephrase it in a manner that attenuates the intensity of emotion, for instance, 'I am currently experiencing a sensation of tension that, in the past, I would have attributed to a craving for a cigarette.'" "I want to smoke" conveys the same meaning. Examining the emotional response mitigates its intensity and facilitates the recognition that one's distress is not genuinely attributed to a craving for cigarettes.

Do not succumb to the notion that you are only capable of having a single option. Instead, consider the possibility of resuming the habit of smoking. Both propositions hold equal significance.

Abstain from any contemplation of partaking in the act of smoking a cigarette under any circumstances. Alter the mental representation to one depicting cigarettes that are repugnant, uncomfortable, and highly undesirable, resembling your worst smoking experience.

Continuously keep in mind your achievements. Each individual undergoes the healing process at a unique rate. Even on the occasion of your initial day without smoking, even a small amount of money saved can still yield a favorable outcome. Kindly ensure to record them as you encounter them. You will inevitably be astounded by the expeditious manner in which you come to assume the benefits as a matter of course.

Consistently reinforce the belief that you are experiencing profound positivity. Both "I feel terrific" and "Oh, am I ever hurting" are equally straightforward expressions. Simplicity results from the diminished syllabic count. The ideas that you consciously reinforce gradually manifest as truth within your subconscious. To ensure that this sentiment is ingrained in your daily routine, consider inscribing "I am filled with immense joy at the prospect of freedom" on a sticky note and affixing it to your bathroom mirror each morning.

Do not deny yourself the enjoyment of a pleasant experience merely because you have abstained from smoking. Suppose we establish a connection between smoking and finding relaxation while being situated on your porch. One can draw parallels between various aspects and smoking during the initial period of cessation. Minimize the likelihood of experiencing deprivation by promptly addressing the triggers as they occur.

Among them is alcohol. Proceed with caution and deliberation on a catalyst that simultaneously diminishes your inhibitions and impairs your cognitive clarity.

Laugh a lot. When contrasting the act of inhaling toxins with laughter, it becomes evident that laughter is an exceedingly superior, potent, and beneficial form of relaxation.

One must never doubt that the act of smoking a single cigarette will rekindle one's addiction. In light of the numerous instances where individuals have strived to overcome their addiction to smoking, only to experience immediate relapse and subsequent feelings of remorse, it becomes increasingly challenging for one to contest the tenacity of addiction.

This pertains to a principle that does not resemble a legal decree such as the "speed limit," but rather bears resemblance to a natural force like "gravity." It is conceivably feasible to exceed the speed limit without encountering immediate consequences, yet it would be ill-advised to engage in reckless actions, akin to spontaneously parachuting out of an aircraft, solely on the basis of going unnoticed.

Exercise caution in permitting your thoughts to be confined within repetitive and unproductive cognitive patterns. Do not regard surrendering as the ultimate conclusion. It marks the commencement of a fresh, wholesome lifestyle wherein unforeseen opportunities shall manifest. Do not place any credence in the information provided by individuals with substance abuse issues regarding the extent of the harm that has already been incurred. You may have inadvertently inflicted damage, though there is no need to undertake any further actions. Cease repeatedly affirming to yourself that the task at hand is arduous. It necessitates ample dedication and labor, yet every endeavor of value calls for exertion. Each day, you acquire fresh knowledge and achieve proficiency in additional skills. You're carrying it out.

Do not indulge in idealizing the enjoyable moments when you were able to engage in smoking. And refrain from feeling envious of the individuals discreetly smoking outside. Instead, consider what it was like to require a cigarette. If smoking were truly remarkable, you would not have spared it a second thought.

Take a brief moment to recall all the negative information you have encountered regarding the necessity of smoking.

Under no circumstances should you entertain the notion that you might engage in smoking, even if you harbor apprehensions regarding your inclination to do so. One is essentially granting oneself the ability to engage in it, even if the consequence of that permission is subsequently subjecting oneself to self-criticism.

12. It is imperative to constantly bear in mind that you possess authority over the words you speak and the actions you take. You cannot be compelled to engage in smoking unless you make a deliberate decision to do so. Opt for that decision with comprehensive knowledge. Upon extinguishing the cigarette, any fleeting solace it may have offered will dissipate, revealing only a potent substance that revitalizes one's cravings. The sole rationale for succumbing to this habit once more and persisting until one's demise is the resolution for doing so. From my perspective, there is equally no valid rationale for opting for that choice.

Avoid the use of the term "never." It is disconcerting to contemplate the permanent cessation of smoking, which may lead one to yield to temptation out of despair, presuming it to be their final chance. This assumption is unfounded. The vending of cigarettes shall persist on the subsequent day, the subsequent week, and the subsequent year. You're welcome to smoke at any time. You are opting to resume smoking and willingly embracing all the associated adverse consequences.

14. Prior to engaging in smoking, it is imperative to consistently communicate with your social support network through a written message. Once you have made the request, exercise patience until at least three individuals have provided a response to your appeal for aid. The sense of "urgency" to smoke will have diminished before their arrival. If you are away from home and unable to make a post until your return, what course of action ought you to pursue?

Reflect upon the duration of time that you have abstained from smoking. Will a slight extension of time have any significance? Prior to succumbing to a relapse, kindly avail yourself of the support of your friends. Enable your innate capacity for logical reasoning and creative thinking to assume control.

15. Please be mindful of the benefits that exist. In order to assist you in mitigating the inclination to engage in smoking, we recommend that you document or articulate your motivations for ceasing this habit. These explanations may comprise:

• Maintaining good health - Experiencing improved well-being • Nurturing a healthier lifestyle - enjoying enhanced physical and mental state

- Safeguarding your loved ones from the harmful effects of secondhand smoke - Ensuring the well-being of those dear to you by shielding them from the risks of secondhand smoke - Prioritizing the safety and health of your loved ones by preventing their exposure to secondhand smoke - Taking measures to preserve the health and safety of those closest to you by minimizing their exposure to secondhand smoke - Upholding the welfare and protection of your loved ones by reducing their exposure to the hazards of secondhand smoke.

▣ Financial conservation

It should be noted that taking action to combat the urge to smoke is always more favorable than taking no action whatsoever. With each successful resistance against the temptation to smoke, you move one step closer to achieving cessation from cigarettes.

## The Financial Consequences of Smoking
"The Adverse Impact of Smoking on Your Finances" "The Detrimental Effects of Smoking on Your Monetary Situation"

According to the American Lung Association, the average price of a packet of cigarettes in the United States is $5.51. Let us consider the scenario where you are an average tobacco user, consuming half a pack of cigarettes per day. On average, you can expect to expend $84 per month. That amounts to an annual cost of slightly over $1,000! Furthermore, it is evident that if one consumes an entire pack of cigarettes daily, the expenses would double accordingly. It is quite probable that you can contemplate several means of allocating an additional $2,000 annually.

## The Act of Smoking Has Detrimental Effects on Your Social Interactions

Although many individuals initiate smoking for social purposes, they seem to lack awareness regarding the potentially detrimental consequences that may ensue from this choice. If you engage in smoking in the presence of individuals who are sensitive to smoke, concerned about secondhand smoke, or simply bothered by it, they will likely exhibit avoidance behaviors towards you.

In all honesty, many individuals will not deem it necessary to have a smoker examined again. Evidently, it seems that some individuals do not display any concern regarding this matter, a considerable portion of whom are presumably smokers themselves. Regardless, do you genuinely have a necessity to constrain your options in dating?

What is your course of action when you find yourself at a performance venue, a dining establishment, or any other public location, and are suddenly compelled to satisfy a biological need? The "No Smoking" sign serves as a cautionary measure urging you to refrain from igniting any tobacco products. You have two options: either you must depart and consequently forfeit a portion of the enjoyment, or you must exercise self-control and restrain the impulse.

Subsequently, there is the presence of the 'unpleasantness quotient' - that is to say, soiled apparel, putrid transportation, and noxious exhalations.

Smoking has a detrimental impact on your overall well-being

When questioned about whether the design of the tendency towards smoking was flawed, a male interviewee responded, "Not at all. Life is poorly organized when one engages in smoking." This individual, a 49-year-old former smoker, acknowledged that he recognized the need to quit when he realized his entire routine revolved around obtaining his next cigarette and the next pack of tobacco. Irrespective of whether one smokes as a means to alleviate stress, this habitual practice can paradoxically lead to heightened levels of stress.

Are you aware that there exists an entire website dedicated to the various pleasures associated with the act of smoking? The discussions on this website encompass comments by individuals who assert to be satisfied with

Perhaps you encounter an individual who is of middle age or older and engages in smoking, prompting you to reflect upon their situation and remark, "Observe, this person has been smoking for an extensive period of time with no apparent adverse effects." Right?

Might I suggest that you inquire with him? Inquire about his opinion on whether he made a satisfactory judgment.

## Why Do We Smoke?

What is the fundamental essence that drives our inner workings? What factors elucidate human behavior and exert the most significant impact on our actions and decisions, encompassing both virtuous and detrimental outcomes? What are the reasons behind engaging in smoking? What are the reasons for desiring to cease smoking? Why have we not ceased smoking already? What is the reasoning behind our decision to stop smoking at this moment? Which factor governs every aspect of our existence, influencing every decision we undertake?

The solution can be understood as an uncomplicated notion known as the Pleasure and Pain principle, as delineated by Sigmund Freud, with its origins traced back to the time of Aristotle. I have discovered it to be foolproof. It is the ultimate authority or solution. It governs all of our actions, decisions, and conduct. All of our actions, whether initiated or omitted, are subject to its control. It is inherent within us from birth; it is steadfastly woven into the very fabric of our genetic composition. It exerts an influence over us, often without our conscious awareness.

Let me explain. The principle of hedonism posits that individuals, as rational beings, possess an innate inclination to promptly satisfy their essential requirements, thereby obtaining pleasurable sensations as a physiological response. In essence, we endeavor to engage in endeavors, pursuits, or undertakings that evoke feelings of gratification. The principle of pain aversion is the antithesis, positing that in our quest for pleasure, we also strive to steer clear of that which inflicts anguish upon us. In essence, our objective is to steer clear of things, activities, or actions that elicit negative emotions. Consequently, all our actions are governed by the imperative to evade suffering and the pursuit of attaining gratification.

The principle of hedonic gratification/displeasure is among the fundamental mechanisms employed in human behavioral conditioning. If you happen to be a parent, it is likely that you are well acquainted with this phenomenon. An instance of this is seen when a child demonstrates commendable conduct, prompting us to offer rewards in the anticipation that it will encourage the continuation of such positive behavior. On the contrary, in cases of misconduct, we administer disciplinary measures with the expectation of reducing the frequency of improper conduct. Nonetheless, it appears that pain carries greater efficacy as a motivator, prompting us to prioritize the mitigation of distress. As a result, children have a tendency to retain the memory of a physical discipline such as spanking to a greater extent than the experience of receiving a treat like a lollipop.

How does this principle influence our forthcoming conduct and/or choices? Indeed, our foremost concern pertains to our future conduct. We are unable to alter our past actions. We are unable to take any action pertaining to our previous endeavors to abstain. Our primary focus is on abstaining from smoking in the future. Could you please provide an explanation on how this operates?

The resultant gratification or suffering that is foreseen possesses nearly equal influential potency as the actual sentiments themselves, as our attention fixates on the forthcoming rewards or consequences. The nature of our existence is contingent upon our subjective interpretation, regardless of its veracity. There exists a traditional proverb that asserts, "Regardless of whether we hold the belief to be veracious or fallacious, our conviction becomes reality." As a consequence, the influencing factor of expected pleasure or pain plays a significant role in shaping the choices we make for the future. The object of your attention becomes the primary reality of your present experience.

However, it should be noted that the pain/pleasure principle does not necessarily dictate that individuals consistently act in ways that serve their own ultimate benefit. This phenomenon can provide an explanation for the occasional participation in self-destructive behaviors. Once more, it urges us to take action based on what we perceive to be in our utmost personal advantage at any particular moment.

What is the significance or implication of all of this? This signifies that our choices are principally influenced by our emotions, rather than our rationality, predominantly on most occasions. Our choices are predominantly influenced by our emotional states and current circumstances. This elucidates the reason behind our occasional propensity for irrational decision-making, as they are founded upon emotions rather than logical reasoning. It elucidates the reason behind our tendency to procrastinate, as it arises from the circumstance wherein the present discomfort of accomplishing a task surpasses the subsequent gratification of its completion. Consequently, our cognitive processes predominantly revolve around short-term considerations, centering on the potential immediate repercussions that would arise from implementing any alterations. Our current focus lies on what holds the utmost reality to us in the present moment. Hence, the consideration of the enduring advantages resulting from effecting a constructive alteration eludes us presently.

So what was the initial reason behind our initiation of smoking, and what were the underlying factors that prompted us to persist? To put it plainly, the reason is that it elicited a positive emotional response from us. Initially, it bestowed upon us greater enjoyment than discomfort, and we subsequently acquired a routine. What is the rationale behind our decision to cease smoking at this point in time? Due to its lack of efficacy, it is causing significant distress in various aspects of our lives such as relationships, employment, and health, thereby necessitating a change. Rest assured, I possess firsthand experience and understanding of the matter at hand. The practice that previously brought us immense joy has evolved into a detrimental influence in our existence. We inadvertently found ourselves entangled in the monotonous cycle of smoking, as days turned into weeks and the habit gradually took hold of us. The concept is simple; we seek that which causes us pleasure, and avoid that which causes us pain.

In the past, we have not ceased the practice of smoking primarily due to the fact that we perceived quitting to be more burdensome than the gratification of living a smoke-free life. The apprehended suffering that results from relinquishing our pursuits engenders transient cognitive deliberation, thereby immobilizing us and rendering us entirely impotent. In a specific instance, the sensation of discomfort associated with cessation becomes more tangible to us than the satisfaction we would derive from abstaining from smoking. However, one must consider the ramifications of smoking, namely the undeniable fact that we are gradually inflicting harm upon ourselves. These thoughts elude us entirely as a result of insufficient concentration and a dearth of consciousness. In that moment, the initial allure of indulging in that first inhalation eclipses the ACTUAL detrimental effects on one's well-being caused by smoking. Take, for instance, the approximate 15-year reduction in lifespan associated with smoking.

On the contrary, have you ever refrained from indulging in smoking? I am aware that you possess such knowledge. How did you accomplish it? What happened? What area did you specifically concentrate on? I shall proceed to recount the events that transpired. You paid attention to the detrimental effects of smoking, the suffering it has inflicted upon you previously, and the inevitable anguish it will bring upon you in the future. During that particular juncture, the actual discomfort associated with smoking surpassed the anticipated gratification that the cigarette could offer. Your focus changed.

Comprehending the pain/pleasure principle is the key to a significant advancement; it is of utmost importance. There exists wisdom in consciousness, and you have now acquired an awareness that all our actions are governed by our inclination to evade suffering and our pursuit of attaining happiness. This elucidates the reasons behind your initiation of smoking, your persistent adherence to this habit well beyond its advisable duration, and your current desire to put an end to smoking. It is evident that pain possesses a greater capacity to drive individuals, thereby leading them to exert considerable efforts in order to circumvent any sources of pain. Additionally, you are aware of the reason why you have not ceased smoking hitherto; regrettably, the act has been strongly linked to negative experiences, causing considerable distress.

Allow us to switch our focus temporarily and delve into a discussion regarding the Tobacco Industry, specifically the deceptive tactics employed by this sector in order to endorse their product.

Tobacco Industry Marketing

Tobacco products are extensively promoted and advertised among consumer goods in the United States. In the year 2006, according to the most recent information accessible, the five leading tobacco companies collectively allocated a sum of $12.49 billion, which amounts to an expenditure of over $34 million dollars on a daily basis, solely for the purpose of promoting and advertising their tobacco products.

In 2009, the U.S. Food and Drug Administration (FDA) obtained substantial jurisdiction over tobacco products, thus potentially altering the future landscape of tobacco product marketing. Nevertheless, it is worth noting that solely North Dakota is allocating funds to its tobacco control program in accordance with the recommended level set by the Centers for Disease Control and Prevention (CDC) in FY2010. This indicates that the promotional endeavors of tobacco companies are taking place without facing substantial opposition from adequately financed state tobacco control programs.

On what areas do the leading cigarette companies allocate their advertising expenditure?

The most dominant category of advertising expenses in 2006, by a considerable margin, consisted of remunerations provided to cigarette retailers or wholesalers in exchange for price reductions on cigarettes offered to consumers. This specific category constituted a total of 73.7 percent, amounting to $9.21 billion, of the overall expenses.

Promotions that added retail value, including "buy one, get one free," as well as coupons for discounted cigarettes, ranked as the second and third highest expenditures, respectively.

The pricing of cigarettes exerts a highly substantial impact on the prevalence of tobacco use among young individuals. A 7 percent decrease in youth consumption is observed with each incremental 10 percent rise in cigarette prices. Hence, reductions in pricing and the implementation of additional value-added promotions at retail stores can counterbalance the effects of incremental state taxes on cigarettes.

What are the implications of tobacco product advertising on the prevalence of smoking among young individuals?

According to a publication in the May 2007 edition of the journal Archives of Pediatric and Adolescent Medicine, it was observed that retail cigarette marketing had a direct impact on the likelihood of adolescents initiating smoking. Furthermore, pricing strategies employed by tobacco companies were found to play a role in increasing rates of smoking across different stages, encompassing initial experimentation to consistent smoking habits. Another factor that was identified as contributing to youth transitioning from experimental smoking to regular daily smoking was the presence of cigarette promotions.

In accordance with the findings of a study published in the American Journal of Preventive Medicine in 2002, it was established that adolescents demonstrating high susceptibility to tobacco advertising and harboring the belief that quitting at any time is possible, exhibited an increased propensity to transition from mere experimentation to habitual smoking.

In the 2001 monograph titled "Changing Adolescent Smoking Prevalence," the National Cancer Institute conducted an assessment of the evidence pertaining to the impact of tobacco advertising and promotional efforts on the initiation of youth smoking. Following the examination of various studies, the National Cancer Institute determined that the research unequivocally supports a cause-and-effect relationship between tobacco marketing and the initiation of smoking among young individuals.

www.ingramcontent.com/pod-product-compliance
Lightning Source LLC
Chambersburg PA
CBHW050249120526
44590CB00016B/2277